Madame Melville

Richard Nelson's plays include *Goodnight Children Everywhere* (Royal Shakespeare Company, Playwrights Horizons, 2000, Olivier Award for Best Play), *James Joyce's the Dead* (Broadway, 2000, Tony Award for Best Book of a Musical), *The General from America* (RSC, Alley Theatre), *New England* (RSC, Manhattan Theatre Club), *Misha's Party* (co-written with Alexander Gelman for the Royal Shakespeare Company and the Moscow Art Theatre), *Columbus and the Discovery of Japan* (RSC), *Two Shakespearean Actors* (RSC, Lincoln Center Theatre), *Some Americans Abroad* (RSC, Lincoln Center Theatre), *Sensibility and Sense* (American Playhouse Television), and *Principia Scriptoriae* (RSC, Manhattan Theatre Club). *Advice to Eastern Europe* (Radio 4) and *The American Wife* (Radio 3). He has written a television play, *End of a Sentence* (American Playhouse), and a film *Ethan Frome*. Among his awards are the prestigious Lila Wallace Readers' Digest Award in 1991, a London *Time Out* award, two Obies, two Giles Cooper Awards, a Guggenheim Fellowship, two Rockefeller playwriting grants and two National Endowment for the Arts playwriting fellowships. He directed the Broadway production of *James Joyce's the Dead* and the off-Broadway production of *Goodnight Children Everywhere*. He is an Honorary Associate Artist of the RSC.

RICHARD NELSON

Madame Melville

faber and faber

First published in 2000
by Faber and Faber Limited
3 Queen Square London WC1N 3AU

Typeset by Country Setting, Kingsdown, Kent CT14 8ES
Printed in England by Mackays of Chatham plc, Chatham, Kent

A CIP record for this book
is available from the British Library

ISBN 0-571-20794-4

2 4 6 8 10 9 7 5 3 1

For Michael Nelson

Madame Melville was first performed at the Vaudeville Theatre, London, on 18 October 2000, produced by Ostar Enterprises, Gregory Mosher, Freddy DeMann, Andrew Fell, and Adam Kenwright. The cast included:

Carl Macaulay Culkin
Claudie Irene Jacob
Ruth Madeleine Potter

Director Richard Nelson
Set Designer Thomas Lynch
Costume Designer Fotini Dimou
Lighting Designer Peter Mumford
Sound Designer Scott Myers
Associate Director Colin Chambers
Movement Jane Gibson
Voice Work Andrew Wade
Stage Management Michael Townsend, Andrew Ralph, Vicki Warwick

Characters

Carl
Claudie
Ruth
Father

MADAME MELVILLE

One can take all possible liberties of line, form, proportions, colours to make feeling intelligible and clearly visible.

Pierre Bonnard

*An apartment. Paris. 1966. Exit to the hallway and
front door, another to kitchen, a third to bathroom and
bedroom. Bookcases, record player and record albums,
etc.*

*Carl, a fifteen year-old American, reads to the
audience from a small paperback:*

Carl

'because she hath
A lovely boy, stolen from an Indian king . . .
And she perforce withholds the loved boy,
Crowns him with flowers and makes him all her joy.'

(*He closes the book, and puts it back in the bookcase.*)
I think I was nearly thirty before I saw an actual stage
production of *A Midsummer Night's Dream*. (*The book
is replaced, he turns back to the audience.*) The young
man speaking to you is the same age I was in 1966.
When I last visited this room. Which long ago ceased to
exist. Today I am a man myself, with wife and children –
one nearly fifteen himself – but I could not find it in my
imagination to see myself, to place the man I am today
here. In this room. For when I think of her, or when
I speak of her, in the middle of a thought, in the middle
of a dream, I am forever – a boy of fifteen. With a voice
like this boy's – honest, simple, thoughtful, and not yet –
uncertain. The uncertainty – that happened here. (*He
looks over the room one more time, then:*) Recently
I came across an interesting discussion of that word by
a professor in New Jersey. 'Uncertainty', he said, is the
tentativeness created from seeing many things from
many points of view.

Short pause.

Uncertainty then is one of the first essential steps toward becoming a writer.

Beat.

The simple facts first. (*He smiles at the irony of this.*) What a devious, insidious phrase. (*then, continuing*) Anyway – we arrived in Paris in the winter, 1966.

Beat.

1966. When you felt the world about to burst its seams. They hadn't snapped yet, but you couldn't help but feel – any time.

Beat.

1966. My father, a businessman, had already been here six months, and when his project expanded we were brought over as well – my mother and me. My brother was at Cornell, smoking pot, he later confessed. And I was enrolled in the American School where I was taught literature by Mme Melville. I wasn't a very good student and hated Paris which seemed – with its streets, its monuments and its people – to make me feel stupid. I had few friends and with those I tagged along on Fridays to the Bus Palladium where – and this was supposed to excite me – we could dance like in America.

Beat.

It was at the Bus Palladium that I first heard the name the Rolling Stones – and where I first watched a young bearded American enthral a crowd of French girls as he burned what I learned through a series of breathless whispers was his draft card. Though when I saw this same young man burn it again another night, one had to wonder.

Beat.

Then, one day, out of the blue, Mme Melville, who had hardly seemed to notice me in her class, asked – if I'd care to join her and the small group of students who met twice a week to see and discuss the very latest films. (*He closes his eyes and recites.*) *Masculine Feminine. Jules and Jim. Hiroshima mon Amour. Blowup. King of Hearts.* (*Opens his eyes.*) It's where I saw my first naked women – my first *moving* naked women – in these films.

Beat.

We'd all meet at her apartment. (*Gestures 'here'.*) I'd return there as well for chocolates or cocoa or tea. She'd always put music on.

The record-player arm suddenly moves, a record falls, and begins playing a puece by Bach.

Music I was careful not to admit not knowing. Music so beautiful . . . Music I had to ask, I had to wonder, why did I not know such music? There was never any music in my house – only what my brother played on his record player. So I knew only that. I had never in my life been to a concert – of such music. The other students in the film group talked about how they liked so-and-so's version of this-or-that better than someone else's version, and I tried to agree. Tried to smile knowingly, but not too aggressively as I did not wish to be actually brought into the conversation. (*Turns and looks.*) And there were books – books upon books, bookcases filled with books. Both here and in her bedroom. In Mme Melville's bedroom. (*Gestures.*) Through there.

Beat.

I looked at all these books, and while others around me discussed what was in them – they had read them! – I – I touched them.

Short pause. The Bach continues to play

And so it was on one Friday evening, in early summer, with school nearly over for the year, that we watched a film about American surfboarders travelling the world looking for big waves, and we strolled as a pack back through the ghost-lit Paris streets, past the gates of the Sorbonne, and up the wiry toy elevator until we were here, where I, while in the toilet, heard first the doorbell, then voices, and the group's loud and many goodbyes.

From the hallway door, we hear these 'goodbyes' off.

And found myself suddenly in the middle of her living room, alone. So I picked up my jacket to go . . .

Claudie Melville, French, thirties and very attractive, enters from the hallway. Carl pretends to be finishing zipping up his fly.

Claudie (*surprised*) You're still here, Carl? You're not leaving with – ?

Carl (*over this*) Where are the others? I was – (*Gestures toward the toilet.*)

Claudie That was Sophie's mother. She was early. Were you getting a ride with – ?

Carl They live on the other side –

Claudie (*over some of this*) That's right. You're the one who takes the Metro. You live in the other direction. Whereabouts do you – ?

Carl Sixteenth –

Throughout this Claudie has appeared very distracted.

Claudie (*not listening*) Have some chocolates. No one ate any chocolates.

Carl I did.

Claudie Then have some more.

She takes a chocolate. Picks up a pile of mail, looks through it, sighs.
   Carl watches her for a moment, then:

Carl I should go.

She turns and looks at him.

Claudie Sophie's mother came too early.

Carl (*explaining*) The Metro closes in –

Claudie Not yet. You've got a little bit of time. (*Continues to look through her mail, then looks up.*) Unless there's someplace you have to . . .

Carl No.

Claudie (*finishing with her mail*) Or I can drive you home. (*She sets the mail down, looks at him and smiles.*) And take off that tie. I detest ties on boys. And push back your hair. Straight back.

He does.

That's better. (*She goes to him and holds his hair back.*) I'm going to have a wine. What about you? Coca-Cola? Orangina? Mineral water? (*She heads for the kitchen.*)

Carl I'll have wine too.

She turns back to look at him, he pretends to look at her books.

Claudie If there's anything that interests you . . .

He looks up confused.

Take what you want.

Still confused.

Borrow a book.

He understands. She goes to the albums and pulls out one and hands it to Carl as she heads for the kitchen:

Claudie Put that on, will you please, Carl?

She goes, the Bach continues.

(from the kitchen) Did you see Lucy's skirt? Did you notice that? Of course you noticed that. You're a boy! The school rule says across the top of the knee. She must have rolled it up during the film. Is that what she did? You were sitting next to her.

Carl *(calls to the kitchen)* No. No, I wasn't. That was Robert.

Claudie *(entering with a glass of wine and a glass of Orangina)* Robert? Then perhaps *he* rolled it up.

Carl I don't think –

Claudie Here *(the Orangina)*. I thought William was Lucy's boyfriend. That's not what I was feeling tonight. What happened to the – *(record)*

Carl I'm sorry . . .

As he puts on the new album:

Claudie Skirts are going way way up. That's what everyone's saying. Inches. Out of sight! As you Americans say. *(She smiles at him.)* Soon, you men will say – why bother. Right?

Before he can respond, the music comes, on: Stephane Grappelli.

Sh–sh. *(She sits on the sofa, kicks off her shoes, closes her eyes.)*

Long pause.
   Claudie is lost in thought, as she sips her wine and gently sways to the jazz.

8

Carl watches her closely, then after a while takes out a new, unopened packet of cigarettes. He hesitates, then:

Carl Cigarette?

She opens her eyes and looks at him.

Claudie (*with a half smile*) I didn't know you –

Carl I do. (*He doesn't.*)

She hesitates, then leans over him, puts her hand on his thigh for balance and takes a cigarette. She lets him light it. The music continues. She looks at his face, then brushes back his hair again.

Carl It doesn't stay.

Claudie It will. We need to train it, so that after a while it won't dare not to. (*Smiles, smokes.*) What did you think of the film tonight?

Carl Not very much.

Claudie Because it was American?

Carl Why would that matter?

She shrugs.

I just got bored. A film about guys surfing . . .

Claudie It's very popular with the kids.

Carl I'm not a kid.

Claudie No.

Beat.

I liked seeing the boys in their bathing suits. That kept me interested. It kept the girls interested. Sophie says she's going to go back and see it again. And bring her mother. (*Laughs lightly.*)

Carl (*still serious*) I liked the films we've been seeing. The more serious ones.

Claudie This was serious.

Carl A bunch of rather thick guys going surfing.

Claudie About a bunch of 'guys' searching, Carl. On a quest – for that one perfect wave. It was mythological. Homeric. But not for you. Fair enough. You liked the French films about sex.

Carl They're not about –

Claudie How well are you doing in your other classes, Carl? I haven't heard about any problems, still –

Carl I'm fine.

Claudie You're a bright boy.

Carl Thank you.

Claudie You could do better in my class.

Beat.

You could speak more.

Carl I pay attention.

Claudie That's not what I said – I said you could assert yourself more. We'd all like to know what you're thinking. (*changing the subject*) I think Lucy's getting set to dump William. And I think it was for Robert that she was raising her skirt. What do you think?

Carl (*after a beat*) I think it doesn't have to be *for* anyone. That's not how everything always is.

Claudie I think you're wrong there. I think I'm right.

They listen to the music.
She sips, takes a puff, then as if suddenly realizing:

Did you stay in the toilet until the others had left? Is that what you were doing?

Carl I didn't hear –

Claudie You didn't hear the bell? You didn't hear Sophie's very loud mother?

Carl (*over this, too emphatic*) No. No!

Claudie You didn't know everyone was leaving?

Carl No! (*He stands.*) I should go.

Claudie You weren't trying – on purpose – to stay behind? I think you were, Carl. And – I think there is nothing remotely wrong with that. (*He is frozen in place.*) But then again maybe you didn't know why you were staying back. I think men often don't know what makes them do the things they do. I think that is why women find men so – dangerous.

    Beat.

And so – terrible. (*She is lost in her thoughts for an instant, then:*) And of course men find women dangerous for totally different reasons. Isn't that true? (*Smiles, sort of teasing, sort of flirting.*) We were talking about just this in class this week, weren't we? Drink your Orangina. (*He takes the glass and drinks, she continues without a beat.*) The books women have written about men – such as they are, and those by men about women. How different they are. It wasn't exactly on the curriculum, I snuck it in. Very bold of me, wasn't it? I looked to you two or three times in the discussion to join us. To tell us what you know about what men think about women. You must know a lot.

    Beat.

Don't you?

He sits back down and drinks his Orangina. As she continues, he fiddles with the magazines etc. on the coffee table.

Next time – participate. Still I'm so happy you're in my class. So nice to see your attentive face there. Though I keep wanting to push that hair back.

She smiles. He looks up and half smiles. He has his hand on a magazine.

Look at that. Have you seen it?

Carl (*looking at the magazine*) No.

Claudie High school kids published that. From Pavini High School – do you know where –?

Carl No.

Claudie *La Zanzara*. Do you know what it means?

Carl The mosquito.

Claudie Very good. Nice name for a student –

Carl I don't think so.

Claudie You haven't read – It's been in the news. Been all sorts of arguments – They discuss divorce, birth control, sexual education. High school students. Like you. The world is changing fast. If you wish to borrow that.

Carl I don't.

Short pause. He puts the magazine down, picks up a book.

Claudie That's right. It's not exactly your kind of thing, is it?

Carl What do you mean?

Claudie I mean – you wish to be a writer yourself, don't you?

Beat.

A poet, isn't it?

No response.

(*as if responding to his question*) Who told me? Did Lucy tell me? (*She smiles.*) I think it was your father who told me.

Carl I didn't know you'd ever met my father.

Claudie Before you enrolled. He came to school to discuss you before he'd enroll you. We had a nice talk.

Carl He's never said he'd met you.

Claudie Why would he? Do you talk about me at home?

Beat.

And he might not even remember me. He saw so many teachers that day. But I remember very well him saying his son wanted to be a poet. And then he laughed. I didn't like your father.

Beat.

I said to him that the world needed all the poets it can get. How come you haven't shown me any of your poems? What are they about?

Beat.

Lucy?

Beat.

You *were* sitting next to her, Carl. You were sitting on her left. And I watched you manoeuvre to make sure you did too.

Carl Like I 'manoeuvred' to stay behind here?

Pause.

Claudie I'll tell you a funny story I heard on the radio. Hand me another of those (*cigarettes*). And look through (*record albums*) – if there's something you want to . . . (*hear*)

> *She lights her cigarette and puts her feet up on Carl's chair, against his leg.*

This man's a novelist. He's written maybe three or four published novels. One day he's riding the Metro and he sees the man next to him reading one of his books. He checks out what page he's on. Eighty-three. Well, he knows for sure there is a very funny incident on page eighty-nine. So he waits. He goes past his stop and waits. Then while the man is on page eighty-nine – the author watches him laugh out loud.

> *Beat.*

Then and there the writer decided to give up novels and write plays. (*Laughs.*) He needed an audience! So don't be a poet, Carl – be a playwright! (*Finishes her wine.*) I think we all need audiences, don't you? I was thinking getting our drinks – by the way there's more Orangina if –

Carl I drink wine.

> *Beat.*
> *She gets up and heads for the kitchen.*

Claudie I was thinking when I was in the kitchen, how nice – (*She is off and continues, off.*) – it is that you did stay back tonight. I really didn't feel like sitting here alone. (*She returns with a bottle of wine and a glass for Carl. For a moment as she sits she is lost in her thoughts, then:*) Sophie's mother came about a half an hour early.

14

Do you know Sophie very well? The conferences I have had about Sophie – I shouldn't be telling you this. (*She pours the wine.*) She's a real bitch. Not like your Lucy. Cheers. Or what do you say in America?

Carl I don't know.

She sits back down on the sofa and draws her feet up under her. Carl takes his wine. She sips hers, looks around, somewhat distracted, then noticing the magazine again:

Claudie So that high school magazine doesn't interest you.

Pause. The music is over. There is a silence in the room. Claudie doesn't know what to say, then:

Claudie Be a playwright! (*Toasts him, then finally:*) Now you say something.

Carl (*after a beat*) I did stay back on purpose. I waited in the toilet until I heard they were gone.

Puffs her cigarette, then:

Claudie Don't be too honest, it's not attractive.

He turns away, hurt.

But on the other hand, don't always just accept what a woman says. She's not always saying everything she means and that, I think it's fair to say, is an understatement. So – one can, a man can laugh at what she says. Put her in her place. No woman wants to be boss all of the time.

Beat.

It's your conversation now. Lead away. (*She waits, watches him, then:*)

Carl Are you a Catholic?

Claudie (*not what she expected*) Why do you –?

Claud The cross. (*around her neck*) And I saw on the toilet wall –

Claudie Yes, I'm a Catholic.

Claud Do you go to Mass?

Claudie I have.

Claud Could I go with you sometime?

Claudie You want to become a Catholic?

Carl I want to go to a Mass.

> *Beat.*

There's a writer I like. A poet. I've been reading about him. He became a Catholic. So I'm interested in –

Claudie Not all good poets become Catholics.

Carl I know –

Claudie Not all poets who become Catholic are good –

Carl I know that, Mme Melville!

> *It is the first time he has used her name this evening. And the formality stops the conversation and changes its tone.*

Claudie (*quietly*) You don't go to any church?

Carl My parents do. I don't.

Claudie Does that trouble them?

> *No response.*

Anything else? It is still your conversation.

> *Beat.*

And yes, I will take you to Mass if you wish. But let me give you a little advice. When you are alone with a girl, don't, right off, start talking about religion. (*She smiles.*)

Carl Am I with a girl now?

She stops smiling.

Claudie No. No, you're not. (*Claudie leans over and looks through the albums. Without looking at him*) Did you like the Grappelli?

No response.

We've just been listening to Stephane Grappelli.

Carl I don't know what I like yet.

She continues to look.

How could I? And yes, I would very much like to borrow some books. That's why, to tell the truth – I stayed behind tonight. To see if I could –

Claudie (*without looking at him*) Please. Look.

Carl And the reason I hardly speak in school or here – or at the films – is because I don't have anything that's worth saying.

Claudie I doubt if you believe that.

Carl It's true. If you could hear some of my thoughts. Some of the things I've almost said? (*He tries to laugh.*) I laugh at myself all the time. Better me than you.

Claudie I wouldn't laugh –

Carl I'll tell you something that's true. At the beginning of the term, when the class books were handed out? I lined them up in my room at home. And measured with my hands their thickness and told myself – Carl, in a few more months you'll know at least this much. (*Shows the width with his fingers.*)

Claudie I'm not laughing. But speaking to you as a teacher now –

Carl How else have you been speaking?

Claudie (*over the end of this*) I would ask you, when you hear a new piece of music or see for the first time a great painting – not to worry how many 'inches' of knowledge is that? I'm saying, Carl, that perhaps it's not something that needs to be measured.

He looks at her, then continues:

Carl In class last week you spoke about rhyme. How in English, because there aren't so many words that rhyme, when one does it's to show off – your mind, your cleverness. Whereas in French, with so many, you rhyme as the heart pumps, as you breathe, as the eyes blink.

Claudie I must be a better teacher than I thought, none of you seemed to be –

Carl I don't know what you mean. It doesn't make sense to me. (*Recites.*)
    'Oui, puisque je retrouve un ami si fidèle,
    Ma fortune va prendre une face nouvelle.'
(*Explains.*) The opening of *Andromaque*.

Claudie Yes. (*She smiles.*)

Carl I learned it so I could speak as one breathes, as one's eyes close and shut. (*Continues.*)
    'Et déjà son courroux semble s'être adouci
    Depuis qu'elle a pris soin de nous rejoindre ici.'

Claudie Good for you, Carl. You should recite for the class –

Carl No. You talked about reading Proust? I've never read a word he's written.

Claudie You're young. You will.

Carl You said, Mme Melville, that to read Proust you must prepare as though for your honeymoon, when one knows that over a period of days two lifetimes will be for ever entwined, joined together, where passion spent only sows more passion and more nights together, and mornings, and long, grey afternoons.

Beat.

What does that mean? I really want to know what that means. Every day I notice things, Mme Melville. Every day I hear myself speak, think – I want to know. I write down notes, I imagine asking you.

Beat.

Claudie Ask me.

Carl *The Magic Flute*. What's it about? What does it sound like?

Claudie That's easy, I have the album here.

Then before she can look:

Carl William Faulkner.

Claudie Yes?

Carl I bought a book. I can't figure it –

Claudie Which one?

Carl I don't know how to pronounce it. *Absalom –* (*He mispronounces it.*)

Claudie Let me loan you another. That's the hardest, I think.

Carl (*onto the next*) The painting in your hallway. The women in the bathtub.

Claudie The print.

Carl (*over this*) Whose is it?

Claudie (*going to the bookcase*) Pierre Bonnard. I have a book.

She finds the book

Carl You said in class one day that you'd been an actress –

Claudie For only a year, years a –

Carl And singer. (*She brings the book back and sets it down.*) And just before Easter you sang a song. What was that song?

Claudie It was just before Lent. And we'd had wine in the faculty lunchroom –

Carl What is the song, Claudie?

His saying her first name stops her.

I'm sorry I –

Claudie No. Don't be sorry. I like my name.

Claudie hesitates, then quietly sings a short bit of an Edith Piaf song. She suddenly stops, turns and rubs Carl's hair.

I think the Opera House will be doing *The Magic Flute*. Let me take you.

Carl (*on to another question*) In the toilet – on the walls. You did that? It's a collage?

Claudie Yes, I suppose so. It's –

Carl From books. Postcards. Magazines. You did that?

Claudie I did.

Carl Of naked men and women.

Claudie Mostly.

Carl And words. You also cut out of –

Claudie It's supposed to be – fun. Funny. Something to look at in the toilet. Is that what kept you in there? The naked women – ?

Carl It's not important then.

Claudie No, it –

Carl I'm not missing something?

Claudie It is not – It's meaningless, Carl. It was done for – to be funny.

Carl (*having picked up the art book*) *Pierre Bonnard.* Is he important?

Claudie He is to me.

Carl Why?

Beat.

You don't know why?

Claudie I know why.

He looks at her

Because there was a man – this was years and years ago – and he took me to a gallery. We first had lunch, then we passed the gallery where there was an exhibition of Bonnard. He took me in, we went from painting to painting. I remember each painting. I remember him holding with his hand my arm, and steering me from painting to painting, and asking me – what do I think? What does it make me feel? What do I see? (*She turns a few pages in the book.*) We went back out into the bright sunlight. It was June. Like now. We went to his apartment. And we made love. We then lived together for nearly three years.

They look at the book.

Carl Is this the book from that exhibition?

Claudie No. I didn't have money then to buy art books. I bought this later.

They turn pages, then:

Carl And if you hadn't gone with this man that day to this exhibition, you wouldn't think Bonnard important?

Claudie Probably not. Certainly not in the same way.

They look at one picture.

What do you see? (*She takes his arm.*) What does it make you feel?

He looks at her, then back at the picture.

Carl A woman after a bath. A nude woman.

Beat.

She is rubbing, cleaning her thigh with a cloth? One foot on a stool – no, it's a chair. She's wearing green shoes or slippers. She's looking down.

Claudie What makes you say she has taken a bath?

Carl Because the water's in the tub. She wouldn't let the water sit there and get cold. She'd get in.

She smiles.

What? Why is that funny –?

Claudie Not funny. I think maybe I said almost the same thing to my teacher. We are two practical people, Carl. (*She squeezes his arm.*) And I think he smiled at me too.

Carl Your teacher? The man who took you to –

Claudie And he stood me in front of this very painting for a long long time before we spoke. 'Is she alone?' he

22

finally asked me. 'There's no one else in the picture,'
I answered. 'Or,' and he turned and looked at me,
'is someone watching her?' I hadn't thought of that.
'Is she aware that someone is – watching her? The
painter of this picture? Monsieur Bonnard? Perhaps,' he
continued, looking back at the painting, 'the bath has
been run for *him*. Perhaps,' he continued now putting
his arm around my shoulder, (*She puts her arm around
Carl's shoulder.*) 'she has left their bedroom, walked
naked as we now see her, her green slippers clapping
upon the hard wood floor or whispering across the
carpet, her toes cracking as she passes their dishevelled
bed and into the hallway, and into – here. Her mission:
to run *him* a bath. And so now, as she waits, she cleans
herself of their lovemaking. Cleans off the 'him' that got
onto her. While he, standing naked unseen in the
doorway, watches.'

   *Pause. They look at the painting. Her arm is still
   around him.*

And then my teacher said, 'It may not be what Bonnard
intended, Mlle Melville. But it's what being here with
you has let me see.'

   Short pause.

Twenty minutes later we're in his bed making love.

   They look at the picture, then she turns the page.

(*about the next painting*) With this I only see fruit in a
bowl on a table. Nothing else. (*Suddenly hears something.*)
Sh–sh. (*Listens, then:*) I thought it might be Ruth. She
lives next – (*door*). (*She gestures.*) But it's from upstairs.
(*She takes his hand in hers and listens, then, in a whisper:*)
An old man lives up there. I think he works in a publishing
office. He's heavy and he walks like – (*Mimics with
heavy steps.*) But some days – nights – one hears –
(*Mimics light steps.*) Listen.

He tries to listen, but she now gently rubs his back.

A young woman, Carl? A young man? Definitely two different sets of steps. But I have never seen anyone but the gentleman on the stairs. (*half to herself*) You hear sounds – you can imagine all sorts of things. Things people are doing. (*suddenly back to Ruth*) Ruth's out on a – What time is it? She should be – (*Looks at Carl's watch.*) Oh God, look at the time! (*Suddenly stands.*) Carl, when's the last Metro?

Carl (*at the same time*) I think I've – (*missed it*).

Claudie (*at the same time*) You haven't missed the last Metro?

Carl It's too late.

Claudie (*over this*) How could we be so stupid!

Carl I'm sorry to make you drive me.

Claudie But I can't drive you.

Carl You offered – You said –

Claudie (*over some of this*) When did I –? I wasn't thinking. My car's in the garage, Carl. I told you that. I told you that when we were waiting on line at the film.

Carl That's right. You did.

Beat.

I'll walk home then. (*He looks at Claudie.*)

Claudie You can't walk to the Sixteenth, Carl.

Carl Why not?

Claudie What about a taxi?

At first neither has an answer for this.

Claudie I'll phone your mother, she'll have to drive over and –

Carl She doesn't drive at all in Paris.

Claudie I think you told me that.

Beat.

And your father – won't be home yet?

Carl He's entertaining business friends. They could be out half the night.

Beat.

Claudie What do we do? (*then the answer about the taxi*) I don't have money for a taxi to –

Carl Neither do I.

Beat.

Claudie What are we going to do?

Beat.

Carl I don't know.

Claudie rubs her head.

Claudie I feel so stupid. I feel responsible –

Carl You're not responsible for me. I'm not a child.

She looks at him.

Claudie No. No, you are not. (*She smiles.*) There's the couch. You could stay here on the – It's not too comfortable. But what would your mother –?

Carl I don't want to be any trouble.

Claudie It is my fault.

*They look at each other. The entire previous
'conversation', has almost been spoken in quotes.*

And you would be no trouble.

Carl I'll leave early. When the Metro –

Claudie Right after breakfast. First let me give you
breakfast.

They look at each other, then:

Carl I'll call then . . . My mother.

*Claudie looks at him, shrugs: 'What else can we do?'
Carl goes to the phone and dials.*

(*into the phone*) Hello Mom? I've missed the last subway.
We got talking and – That's a lot of money to waste
on – Mme Melville's said I could stay on – their couch.
I've said that. She says – Here, Mom, she wants to talk
to you.

*He holds out the phone. Claudie hadn't wanted to
talk, but now has no choice.*

Claudie (*clears her throat, sets down her wine glass,
then*) Hello? Mrs – No. It is no bother at all. And it is
all my fault. We got to talking about the film tonight
and – Please.

Beat.

I don't mind, I assure you. Yes. I just don't know how
I could be so stupid. Good. I will have him call the first
thing. What? (*She gives Carl's mother her phone number.*)
You're welcome. (*Starts to hang up, then:*) He's a very
good student. You should be proud of him. Goodnight.
(*Hangs up.*) She says it's fine. She doesn't mind.

*Short pause. For a moment neither knows what to
say, then:*

26

Carl A lot of fifteen-year-old boys stay out until God knows when. And with God knows who. At least she knows I'm with my – teacher.

Claudie nods at this thought, suddenly hears footsteps upstairs.

Claudie Listen. The old man's got company. A girl or a boy? What do you think?

Beat.
As they listen:

Sometimes you also hear . . . noises. Let me get some sheets for the sofa.

She goes.

Carl She thinks you have a husband.

Claudie (*off*) What?

Returns with sheets. She looks at him.

Carl She thinks – there's a husband – (*Gestures: 'here'.*)

Beat.

My mother thinks – She asked the other day – if Mme Melville's husband went to the films with us.

Beat.

I think because of the 'Madame'.

Claudie starts to make the bed, Carl tries to help.

Claudie The school asked me to use –

Carl I know.

Claudie And what did you answer? About whether Mme Melville's husband went to the films?

Carl I said – he hasn't so far. I guess he doesn't like films.

She looks at him and smiles.

Claudie (*as they continue*) I don't have men's pyjamas . . .

Carl I don't need –

Claudie I keep a few new toothbrushes – I'll set one out.

Carl (*innocently*) Why do you keep new – (*Stops himself.*)

She watches him as they finish up the bed, pillows, etc. Then, as if out of the blue, to say something:

Claudie School's almost over. What are you doing for the vacation?

Carl My mother and I are going back to the States.

Claudie nods, lights a cigarette, offers one to Carl, who shakes his head, and they continue with the couch, etc.

Claudie (*getting the cigarette*) Whereabouts in the States – ?

Carl Ohio.

Claudie Where's that?

Carl In the –

Claudie Never mind.

Beat.

You looking forward to that?

No response.

I'll miss you. It's late, we should both get to bed. You want to use the bathroom first?

He hesitates, then looks toward the toilet, she stops him.

I might have something you could wear.

Carl I don't need –

Claudie Let me see how –

She measures his shoulders.

Carl (*quietly*) I'm fine in my underwear.

He looks at her, then goes off to the bathroom. Pause. Claudie finishes the last little bit of bed-making, and starts to pick up the wine and glasses, then decides to pour herself another glass.
We hear water running in the bathroom sink.
She sits down on the couch, sips her drink. Her eye catches the Bonnard book, she picks it up and starts to look through it.
Toilet flushes off, and Carl returns:

Carl It's all – (*yours*).

Claudie (*over the book*) I then had to write a paper. My boyfriend who was also my teacher– who had taken me to see – he assigned a paper on art. And I wrote about Bonnard. I described this painting just as he had described it to me.

She turns to Carl, puffs on her cigarette.

I got the paper back, Carl – and it was full of red marks. Where's your critics? Where's your research? Where's your thinking? This is supposed to be an essay not a sentimental journey! (*She smiles, bemused, shakes her head.*) 'Think for yourself,' he wrote, at the top.

She closes the book, Carl tries to smile.

Teachers, right? (*And she sighs.*) You are finished?

He nods.

Anything you need – ?

He shakes his head.

Then – goodnight.

Carl Goodnight.

She stops and goes right up to him, hesitates, then holds out her hand for him to shake.

Claudie Goodnight.

They shake hands and she goes off to the bathroom.
He turns off the lights; light now pours from the hallway and bathroom. In the dark, Carl takes off his pants and shirt and gets under the sheets on the sofa.
Immediately Claudie, still dressed, returns and picks up her wine glass.

('*explaining*') I didn't finish my wine.

She sips. He doesn't move. In the darkness, she sniffles, it is clear that she is trying not to cry. Carl doesn't know what to do, then:

Carl Are you okay?

Claudie Yes. (*She smiles.*) Yes. I am okay. (*She sighs.*) Tonight, I am so happy not to be alone. Thank you. (*She finishes her wine.*) Here. Give me your hand. Give me your palm. (*She sits on the couch and he gives her his hand. She tickles the palm with her finger.*) Do you know what this means? When someone does this to your palm?

Beat.

It means they want to have sex with you. (*She tickles again.*) Like this. So if Lucy ever . . . Now you'll know.

There aren't enough hours in the day to teach everything in school. (*She starts to get up, stops, and suddenly holds out her palm.*)

Want to try it?

> *He is frozen. She gets up, rubs his head and leaves, but immediately returns with a robe.*

Try this on. I think it should fit. Stand up and try it on.

> *Carl hesitates getting out of bed in his underwear, but does, and stands, embarrassed as she first holds up the robe, then puts it on him. Claudie stands back and looks.*

That's better. In case to have to, now you don't have to walk around here just in your underwear.

Carl (*softly*) Goodnight.

> *He gets back on the sofa under the sheet, still in the robe.*
> *Claudie has gone to the records and begun looking through. After a moment, he half sits up and watches her, then:*

Claudie Will this (*music*) bother you? I don't want to keep you up.

Carl No. It won't bother me.

Claudie Sometimes music helps me get to sleep.

> *Beat.*

Carl (*quietly*) Me too.

> *She puts on an album: more jazz – perhaps Wayne Shorter or Charlie Parker.*
> *Claudie sits on the floor and listens. She moves to the music, closing her eyes.*

*She sips from her drink, as the music plays for a
while. Suddenly she stands up, startling Carl.*

Claudie (*standing*) I know something you would be
interested in. You weren't asleep?

He shakes his head.

There's a book – Come on. Get up. (*She starts to pull
him up.*)

Carl Where are we – ?

Claudie (*over this*) I want to show you this book. It's in
my bedroom.

Carl What sort of –

Claudie (*over this*) Sh–sh. (*referring to the music*) Listen
to that. I love that. Don't you love that. You are sleeping
in the robe, Carl? How funny you are. You are very
funny. Please, do you wish to see this book or not?

Carl What – ?

Claudie It's an art book, Carl. (*Finishes her wine.*) Come
on. (*She takes his arm and leads him off.*)

Carl (*heading off*) An art book?

They are off.
*The music continues to play. Carl returns, still in his
robe, now holding the 'art' book – an illustrated
Kama Sutra of Vatsyayana.*
*As the jazz continues under him, he speaks to the
audience.*

This was the art book. (*Opens and reads.*) 'Man is
divided into three classes, the hare man, the bull man
and the horse man, according to the size of his lingam.
Women also, according to the depth of her yoni, is either
a female deer, a mare or a female elephant.'

Beat.

'There are thus three equal unions between persons of corresponding dimensions, and there are six unequal unions, when the dimensions do not correspond, or nine in all as the following table shows.' (*He holds up the book to show us the table. Reading again*) 'Equal: Hare/Deer. Bull/Mare. Horse/ Elephant. Unequal – '

Beat.

Well – you can read it for yourself. The book, I've since learned, is readily available. (*Closes the book and goes and turns off the music.*) Anyway, we got to looking at this book in her bedroom and at the artwork which she said had true historical and aesthetic interest.

Beat.

We laid on her bed and looked through the book. On our stomachs. Then she said she *had* to brush *her* teeth and she returned naked and rolled me over onto my back and undid the cord of the robe which I had already tied in a knot by accident.

Beat.

She had a design which ran across the top of her walls – blue and white, a pattern of shapes. I stared at that, then I closed my eyes.

Beat.

I stopped breathing. Or that's what it felt like. I heard every sound. Felt every pump of my heart.

Beat.

She sat upon me. She put me into her. I dared not open my eyes. My arms I kept straight against and alongside my body.

Beat.

She moved and almost instantly it happened. When I felt it, I wanted to let her know so she could move and get off, but she didn't move. It's the one time I opened my eyes. And she was smiling at me.

Beat.

She moved off.

Beat.

I heard her running a bath. She called me.

Claudie (*off, calls*) Carl!

Beat.

Carl The bath, she said, was for me. She stood, foot on chair, cleaning herself. It was years later before I realized what she had been doing – what she was . . . giving to me: that Bonnard painting.

Beat.

She smiled when I came into the bathroom. She winked. And said I was very handsome.

Beat.

She never took off her small silver cross, and it swung across her breasts as she cleaned.

Beat.

In bed I laid on my stomach and tried to sleep. She put an arm over my back, a leg over my thigh, and I'm pretty sure she fell asleep this way. Holding me this way.

Beat.

Again it was years and years before the thought occurred to me that perhaps this is what I gave her – something . . . breathing to hold on to in the night.

Beat.

I watched the dawn break through her white curtains, and still did not move until I felt the light pull, tug, of her fingertips against my bare side, and I then allowed myself to be righted again upon my back, and again she put me inside of her, and it happened all again – quickly.

Beat.

This time I opened my eyes and watched her face in the morning light. Her chin. The curve of her nose. Her mouth. But I tried not to look at any other part of her nakedness. Odd as it sounds, I felt that perhaps I shouldn't. (*Carl begins to dress. As he dresses, he continues.*) The first train was, I think, at around six. But I remembered that she had wanted to give me breakfast.

Beat.

But she forgot about that.

Beat.

I found a roll in the kitchen. I made coffee. I lost myself in her books and records. I tried to stay out of her way, expecting to hear at any moment, 'Carl, shouldn't you be going?'

Beat.

But these words were never said. She never spoke them.

Carl, now dressed, sits on the floor and begins looking through the record albums. Music plays on the record player.
   Pause.
   Knock on the door. Carl turns toward the bathroom, not knowing what to do.
   Another knock, then Claudie, hair wet, in a short robe, appears.

Claudie Could you get that, Carl?

She disappears to dry her hair. Another knock as Carl gets up and goes out to answer the door.
   He returns following Ruth, Claudie's neighbour – American, thirty. She is dressed in messy clothes, her hair uncombed, no make-up, etc.

Ruth You must be one of Claudie's students she's always talking about.

Carl Is she always talking about me?

Ruth I don't know. (*Calls.*) Claudie! (*Turns back to Carl.*) She's not a bad teacher, I hear.

Claudie enters, drying her hair with a towel.

Claudie (*entering*) Where's – ?

Ruth He's just left.

They kiss on the cheeks

I just left him at the corner.

Claudie How did it go? You met – ? (*referring to Carl*)

Ruth Yeh. Hi.

Claudie (*over this*) So what's he like?

Carl (*to Ruth*) Hello.

Ruth We're going to a club tonight. He knows a lot of people in clubs. Are these yours? (*cigarettes*) You don't smoke.

Claudie They're Carl's.

Ruth He sings too. And plays the guitar. (*to Carl, taking a cigarette*) You don't mind?

Claudie (*over this*) Coffee? Carl, do you want coffee?

Carl holds up his cup – he has coffee.

Claudie (*over this*) Ruth's from America –

Ruth (*continuing, not listening*) I think Robert's the first real French man I've found interesting.

Claudie moves toward the kitchen.

I don't want coffee.

Claudie stops. Ruth gestures to Carl – for a light. He picks up matches and lights her cigarette as:

By the way – (*puff*) we heard voices last night in here. We were coming up the stairs. It was late. Was there any . . . ? (*Then she realises that Carl is more than a student and turns to him.*) Oh.

Claudie I'll have one of those too. (*Goes to take a cigarette.*)

Ruth (*looking over Carl*) I'm sorry, I didn't catch your name.

Claudie Carl.

Ruth Carl. How do you do, Carl.

Claudie (*heading for the kitchen*) You're sure you don't want – (*coffee*). (*She is gone.*)

Ruth (*still looking over Carl*) I'm Ruth. I live next door.

Carl I know.

Ruth So you're not one of Claudie's little students.

Carl Actually – I am.

Beat.

One of her little students.

Ruth At the American School –

Carl Yes. (*She stares at him.*) I'm in the tenth grade.

Claudie returns, bowl of coffee in hand.

Ruth (*to Claudie*) He's in the tenth grade.

Claudie (*smiles, sips, then*) We went to see a film last night. A group of students and me. Poor Carl here missed the last train.

Short pause, as they sip, smoke, look back at the album jackets.

Ruth Enjoy the film?

Claudie I did.

Carl It was about surfing –

Ruth (*over this*) So you missed the last Metro. Poor boy.

Claudie And so he had to stay here with me. I fixed up the sofa for him. Didn't I?

Short pause. Ruth watches as Claudie goes over to Carl and kisses the top of his head. He slightly pulls away.

Claudie Don't be embarrassed.

Carl I'm not embarrassed.

Claudie Ruth understands. (*She sits in the chair behind him, rubs his shoulder.*)

Ruth Robert says I should get a bigger bed. (*Then getting 'into' herself and her problems.*) This from a man who says he normally sleeps on the floor – or on one of those thinny thin mattresses from the orient? What are they called? He gets into my bed – but he is a big guy. How tall do you think Robert is?

Claudie I only saw him the one –

Ruth Guess.

Claudie Six –

Ruth Something like that. We didn't wake you? I mean –
he did play me two of his songs at something like four
in the morning. I'm saying – Robert, sh–sh, sing in the
morning. He says – (*French accent*) 'I sing when I feel
like singing.'

  Beat.

I've never seen a naked man strum a guitar before – you
know: bouncing. It's an unnatural sight. He's got a cousin
who has offered him a job. (*more random memories*)
And an uncle who's somehow in the government. They
don't speak. He's been to America twice. Once to Florida
with his parents when he was a boy. Then once to
Manhattan where he bummed around for about three
weeks, living off people he just met, sleeping – wherever.
Once he slept under someone's sink that had a drip.
In the middle of the night, he said, they turned on a light
and there he was trying to fix the drip. He's very handy.
You know my record-player that's been broken for
weeks? He almost got it to work. That's what he said –
he almost fixed it. (*She seems lost in a thought for a
moment, then, changing gears, to Claudie:*) He's really
young. (*to Carl*) Where in America are you from?

Carl Ohio.

Ruth Never been there. I've been to Orlando, Florida.
I've been to pretty much all of the East Coast states
except for Maine and, I think, Rhode Island. I don't
think I've been there. I'm from Montclair, New Jersey,
do you know it? And New Hampshire. I haven't been
there.

Carl No. I don't know it.

Ruth I tell people here that I'm from New York – same
thing. But since you're an American –

Claudie Ruth's been taking classes at the Sorbonne, Carl.

Ruth Among other things. But not officially. But maybe that'll happen. I'm – I just sort of follow the crowds in and sit and listen to – whatever they happen to be teaching that day. You wouldn't believe some of the courses I've been sitting in on – they're all over the map. It's how I met Robert – I was on my way to one of these classes and he was playing his guitar and singing on the Rue des Ecoles. Right around the corner from – (*Gestures.*)

The phone rings. Claudie goes to answer it.

Claudie (*into phone*) Hello? Oh yes. He is. Just a minute. (*Covers phone.*) Carl. It is your father. He has to come into town this morning. He can pick you up.

Holds out phone. Carl hesitates.

Carl I can take the train, he doesn't have to –

Claudie Carl.

Continues to hold out the phone to him. Then as he takes it, she half whispers to him:

I was thinking of going to Le Louvre today. Is that something you'd like to do with me?

He looks at her.

(*Nods to the phone.*) I don't know if it is all right with . . .

Carl (*into phone*) Dad? What? Yes, she told me. Actually – Mme Melville –

Ruth looks at Claudie and smiles as she mouths: 'Madame Melville'.

– is taking a group of students to Le Louvre this – (*Turns to her.*) – afternoon?

40

She nods.

She asked if I – It's fine, Dad. I'll take the train. Dad, she – Yes, he's coming too! Good-bye. Bye! (*He hangs up. Short pause.*)

Claudie I hope I didn't create a problem, Carl.

He shakes his head.

Le Louvre is one of the most important museums in the world.

Carl He knows that. It's fine. I can go.

Claudie Good.

Ruth (*who has been paying close attention*) Who's the 'he' he was referring –

Claudie My husband. Carl's parents are convinced for some reason that I have a husband. I learned this last night, when they allowed Carl to stay . . .

Beat.

I suppose the 'Madame'. Which I use only for school.

No one knows what to say for a moment, then:

Carl He doesn't go to museums himself. They – scare him I think. My father. He doesn't like a lot of things. He doesn't like anything he doesn't understand.

Short pause.

Ruth So you two are going to Le Louvre today. With a group like you – ?

Claudie No. Just the two of us.

Beat.

Ruth I'd come too, but . . .

Claudie But what?

Ruth But you don't want me, do you?

Claudie (*smiling*) No.

Ruth And – what's the time? (*She takes Carl's wrist and looks.*) Jesus, I have a lesson in a minute.

Carl (*to Claudie*) Lesson?

Ruth Maybe I should have some coffee, if it's no –

Claudie (*on her way to the kitchen*) I'm getting it.

She is gone. Ruth sighs.

Ruth (*looking at herself*) These are the clothes I – I almost said that I slept in – but that isn't true. (*Smiles.*) That I wore last night. Just threw them on to go out for breakfast.

Claudie returns with coffee.

(*to Claudie*) I paid for breakfast by the way. My ex-husband would never have let me do that. He'd have broken my arm if I tried to do –

Claudie (*to Carl*) Ruth was married back in –

Ruth Montclair.

Claudie How old is Robert? He looked like he could be –

Ruth Twenty-five? Twenty-eight? Nineteen? I don't know. (*to Carl*) He's not in the third grade so you wouldn't know him.

Claudie smiles at the joke, Carl doesn't.

(*to Claudie*) Since you brought him up –

Claudie Who? Robert or your ex – ?

42

Ruth (*over this*) What do I say about my ex-husband all the time?

Claudie I don't know. So you're talking about your ex – ?

Ruth About both of them. (*Turns to Carl.*) Carl, when we were in school, my ex and me – he was on the track team. And he wore those cute shorts that were really shiny, like fake-silky? You know what I –

Carl They still do.

Ruth He knows them. If it weren't for those shorts!

Sits back, sips her coffee, others wait, then:

(*to Claudie*) I've told you this?

Claudie nods.

(*referring to Carl*) Will he mind if I –?

Claudie No. He won't.

Ruth (*to both of them*) I'm maybe eighteen and I accidentally touch with my hand those shorts. We're talking. Then we're – kissing and I touch.

Beat.

I lost my virginity against those shorts. I lost about eight years of my life because of those shorts. But the point I'm getting to, Claudie, is guess what kind of underwear Robert's wearing?

Claudie Fake-silky?

Ruth I didn't believe it. (*to Carl*) You don't wear fake –?

Claudie (*answering for him*) No. No, he doesn't.

Ruth Oh. Anyway – so why did I bring this up?

No response. She can't remember, but continues.

43

So they're silky, but they are also not too clean, I noticed. You don't think he has any – disease or anything? They really weren't clean. (*Lost in thought for a moment, then:*) Anyway. Thanks for the coffee. (*She gets up, takes Carl's wrist again and looks at his watch.*) They're probably waiting outside my door.

Claudie (*to Carl*) Ruth teaches violin.

Ruth (*kissing Claudie*) Have a nice time at Le Louvre. (*to Carl*) Nice to meet you. (*Whispers to Claudie.*) He's so sweet. (*She goes, then immediately returns.*) They are outside my door. The mother and the student. (*She goes again. Short pause.*)

Claudie That's my neighbour, Ruth.

   Beat.

She's American. (*She rubs his shoulders as he continues to look through albums.*) Like you.

   She hugs him from behind. From off (*Ruth's apartment*), *the sound of a child's violin lesson: start and stop as he/she plays the waltz 'Over the Waves'.*

She's also a very fine player herself. (*Leans over him and points to the albums.*) Keep turning. A few more. There. Take that one out.

   He takes out an album.

That's her. (*Points to a photo.*) That's her all-girl quartet. It's the only album they've made so far. But they're great.

   He looks at the album. Child's lesson continues off.

Carl She didn't act like a . . .

Claudie Like a what?

Carl I don't know. I've never met a musician before.

Claudie They're not all like –

Carl I didn't think –

Claudie But they also don't walk around in black suits and ties and –

Carl I know that.

Claudie Good. I should get dressed. (*She doesn't get up, she reaches and holds back his hair off his face, rubs his head.*) Am I hurting you?

    Beat.

I don't wish to hurt you.

> *She presses her face against the top of his head, sighs, then stands and goes to get dressed.*
>   *Pause. The music lesson continues. Also, slowly, the sounds of the outside begin to be heard – cars, life, street noise.*
>   *Carl speaks to the audience.*

Carl We walked the halls and galleries of Le Louvre for six hours, occasionally resting on a bench, but always in sight of paintings to look at. The greatest paintings, she would say, that the hand of man had ever created.

> *Beat.*
>   *The music lesson begins to fade. Over the course of the speech, outside noise is replaced with echoing inside-the-museum noise – coughs echoing, whispers echoing, footsteps echoing.*
>   *Then they are replaced again by the sounds of outside, along the Seine: traffic, boats, birds, children, etc.*

She had walked these halls many many times before – she had favourites over which she enthused, demanding my enthusiasm. She had loves and she had hates, and she had confusions.

Beat.

She spoke with two paintings as if they were old friends –
or to the people portrayed. I didn't know. She stopped to
let me hear the echoing voices, and steps.

He listens.
Claudie appears in the bedroom doorway, finishing
getting dressed.

Claudie Never close your ears, Carl. The greatest mistake
people make looking at art is to close their other senses.
But paintings live in sound. They live among these
footfalls, that child's cry. That man's cough. Those
sweethearts' whispers.

Beat.

Carl (*continuing to the audience*) She took me to a room
she said she hadn't visited since she was sixteen. It's
known, she said, as a great place where boys can pick
up girls. Along one wall was an Ingres, his huge portrait
called 'Odalisque'. A young naked woman has her back
to us, she is turning, lying, looking sensually at us. Her
skin the colour – and the taste, she insisted – of honey.

Beat.

Girls came here, she explained –

Claudie (*in the doorway, putting on her shoes*) – because
after the boys looked at this Ingres, every girl's ass looks
inviting. (*Claudie disappears back into her bedroom.*)

Carl Two teenage girls sat on a side bench, hands folded
in their laps, giggling. When I turned to look at them,
they stopped and stared down. I felt Mme Melville
stick her finger in my back pocket and pull me away –
jealously, I think. (*He smiles.*) Then as we moved, I felt
her finger stroke back and forth across my butt, inside
my pocket.

Beat.

Not every painting or sculpture in Le Louvre is of a nude. But nearly every one, or perhaps every one, is – of a body. Mme Melville's words.

Beat.

You take away the body, its muscles, its flesh, its sex –

Claudie (*coming out of the bedroom*) – and you empty this building. (*fixing her stockings, brushing her hair, etc., as she prepares to go out*) Carl, a man is not only his sex . . .

Carl She said this as we stared at a painting of a very healthy-looking saint with arrows sticking though his muscular torso –

Claudie (*continuing*) But a man's sex is what makes him a man.

Beat.

Carl I said to her: 'No one ever put it that way in Ohio.'

As Claudie continues to get ready behind him.

One painting confused me. I remember its name – I bought a postcard of it years later. 'Gabrielle d'Estrée and Her Sister'.

Beat.

Two young women are shown naked from the waist up – there's a sort of curtain covering below that. One – Gabrielle or her sister? – has reached over with her hand and is pinching or holding the other's naked nipple. Both look at the artist. At us. What is this about? I asked Mme Melville and she explained –

Claudie The world's a lot more interesting than we give it credit for. (*She disappears into her room.*)

Carl Outside we walked together along the Quai du Louvre. Mme Melville stopped at a kiosk and purchased a small book of paintings from the museum. I watched her take out her money, bending a leg to hold up the purse. The late-afternoon, early summer's sun seemed to touch her and set her apart from the world. As if a sculpture. As if a work of art.

Beat.

I felt more desire than I'd ever in my life felt before.

Beat.

The book was for me. She brushed back her hair, which the wind off the Seine kept blowing across her face. 'A souvenir,' she explained, as she placed it into my jacket pocket. The expression on my face, I think, stopped her, stopped her smiling. And then for the first time, though we had been together all day, all night, in her apartment, in her bed, I reached and I touched her. I touched her arm, and then held it. And I would have kissed her – until then I had never kissed a girl – but I would have kissed her had she not suddenly run off.

Short pause.

She ran to a man I recognised as Monsieur Darc, my mathematics teacher at school. With him was his young daughter holding a balloon. They kissed each other on the cheeks. They spoke. She seemed to talk very sternly at him. They did not kiss good-bye.

Beat.

Walking home she asked if I wanted to stop for coffee. Then she ordered wine. Suddenly it was like I wasn't even there. She found a pair of sunglasses in her bag and put them on. We sat there for a long time. And then we returned to her apartment.

Carl goes to the doorway, and returns with Claudie,
as they enter from their outing to Le Louvre.
Silence. No one speaks.
Carl takes out his new book from his jacket pocket.
Claudie remains distracted.

Carl (*holding the book*) Thank you for the –

Claudie Put some music on, will you?

He hesitates.

What are you looking at? What are you looking at?

Carl (*confused at her outburst*) What kind of music do
you – ?

Claudie I don't care! Something! (*She takes off her
shoes, and heads for her bedroom. As she goes, she
mumbles under her breath:*) Men.

*She is gone. He puts music on. Ruth has entered, she
has changed – looks great, well dressed, hair fixed,
etc.*

Ruth I heard you come in. Is Claudie – ?

*He turns toward the bedroom. As Ruth heads for the
bedroom:*

Can you turn that down? (*the music*)

*He turns it down as Claudie come out, putting on a
sweater.*

Ruth (*explaining*) I heard you come in –

Claudie (*going to Carl*) Why can't you keep that out of
your face? (*A bit aggressively, she pushes back his hair.*)
And I can't hear that.

He turns the music up.

Ruth How was Le – ?

Carl It was great.

Claudie (*over this*) I ran into Paul. And I'm sick and tired of running into Paul. Every day at school I have to run into Paul! There he is with a big smile on his face like nothing has happened! Buying his daughter balloons! (*seeing Carl*) I'm sorry. Carl, you should get home.

Carl Why?

Claudie Why? Because it is time you went home.

Ruth By the way, your mother stopped by, Carl.

Carl My mother?

Ruth She said she was your –

Claudie (*over this*) Did you give your mother my address?

Carl No. I –

Claudie How did she get my address then, Carl?

Ruth She said she called the school.

Claudie It's Saturday. No one's at the school.

Ruth I think she said she got the address from the headmaster at school. So I assumed she had called the –

Claudie She called the headmaster at his home.

Ruth She said she was just in the neighbourhood. I told her you'd probably be back . . . (*Takes Carl's wrist and looks at his watch.*) Soon.

Pause. No one knows what to do.

(*noticing*) You have my album out. Have you been playing –?

Claudie Not yet.

Beat.

Carl wants to hear it.

Pause. The music continues to play.

Ruth (*standing*) I think I'm in the way – I'm sorry.

She heads off. Claudie, hearing something in her voice, calls:

Claudie Ruth? Have you been crying? (*She follows her off. Off*) Are you all right?

Off in the hallway, Ruth bursts out crying. Carl sits and doesn't know what to do. Off, Claudie tries to get Ruth to talk:

What is it? Ruth? Tell me.

Then mumbled talk, and Claudie leads Ruth back into the room and immediately out into the kitchen.

Carl (*as they pass*) What's – ?

They are gone.

Is there anything I can do?

Pause. Music plays. Claudie returns, crosses the room and exits toward the bathroom.

What can I – ?

She is gone. She returns holding a bottle of white liquid.

Claudie (*as she heads back to the kitchen*) She has crabs. (*She stops.*) Robert, the naked bouncing guitar player, gave her crabs. (*She starts to go, then stops.*) You know what crabs are, don't you?

He hesitates.

They're little –

Carl Sure.

She looks at him and goes. A moment later Ruth comes out, followed by Claudie holding the bottle.

Ruth (*entering*) I'll take a shower in a minute. I just got dressed. I don't feel like taking my clothes off yet. Where are those cigarettes?

Carl finds the cigarettes, she goes to get one.

(*to Carl*) They're really disgusting. They look just like little . . .

He slightly moves away.

You don't get them by sitting next to someone, Carl. (*She laughs to herself, then quickly turns to Claudie, wiping the tears off her face.*) How come you have a bottle of stuff for . . . (*Points to the bottle.*)

Beat.

Never mind.

Carl (*to Ruth*) Is that too loud? (*music*)

Ruth What?? Why are French people so unclean?!

Short pause. Claudie is hurt. Ruth realises this. Sighs, then:

Why are men so unclean?

Ruth reaches out toward Claudie who comes and takes her hand and sits with her. Ruth sniffles. Short pause.

Claudie I remember when I had to get that stuff (*the crabs medicine*). You have to get a prescription first. Which I did. I took it to a pharmacy.

Ruth Why didn't *he* get the –

Claudie shrugs and continues.

Claudie I stand in line. I hand the paper to the pharmacist and he says in a loud voice: 'What is this for?'

Beat.

'Crabs,' I half mumble. 'Crabs!' he repeats back. (*in a loud voice*) Then the woman behind me. She's about – (*to Carl*) Probably your mother's age.

Ruth (*trying to joke*) Which is what – your age?

Claudie smiles.

Carl (*joining the joke*) No, Mom's a little younger.

Ruth laughs hard at this.

Claudie She taps me on the shoulder and says, though it says on the bottle to shower twice a day with it, she'd found three times was really needed especially for the men. Because of all the folds and things. I'm serious. Then she stands and sort of mimes a penis – we're in the pharmacy – in line. Stands there – (*Claudie mimes this.*) And she says you have to really check all around it. Lift it up. Look here, there. She said either I should help or he should get his mother.

Laughter. The phone rings. Claudie goes and picks it up, listens for an instant, then:

(*into phone*) Who? I'm sorry. (*She hangs up, goes back and sits down. To Carl*) It was your father.

Short pause. Music plays.

(*to Ruth*) So he gave you crabs.

Beat.

Ruth So you ran into Paul.

53

Carl Is 'Paul' Monsieur Darc?

Ruth That's right. She and Monsieur Darc used to go out together.

Carl But Monsieur Darc is married.

Ruth (*picking up the book on the table*) What's this? The *Kama Sutra*? I didn't know you had this.

Claudie I don't usually keep it out here.

Ruth (*to Carl*) Have you seen this?

He doesn't respond.

Claudie (*to Ruth*) Are you going out with Robert tonight?

She ignores the question.

Then you'll eat with us. Carl and I haven't eaten all day.

Carl Am I staying for –?

Ruth (*suddenly standing*) Carl wants to hear my album. Let's put it on for him! (*Leans over Carl and rubs his head.*) You little music lover, you.

Claudie Ruth, please.

Ruth (*surprised*) I wasn't . . .

Carl has managed to put on the album: an early Beethoven or Mozart.

Ruth How was Le Louvre. Did you show him the pick-up room? Sh–sh. That's me. Hear me?

They listen. Phone rings again. Claudie hesitates, then goes and answers it.

Claudie (*into phone*) Hello? Yes. One moment. (*Covers the receiver.*) It's your mother, Carl.

Carl stands and goes to the phone. Music plays.

Carl (*into phone*) Hello? Yes, I had a great time. Incredible art. (*Beat.*) What time is it now? (*Looks at his watch.*) Actually we all were about to start making dinner. The whole gang here. A French dinner. Monsieur Melville is supervising.

Claudie and Ruth start making background noise of a group of students together. Carl nods to them – louder.

Sorry, Mom, I can't hear. (*to the room*) Hey everyone could you keep it down?

They don't.

What? (*into phone*) Sorry. I have to go. Monsieur Melville needs my help with something! Bye!!

Hangs up. The others are quiet. Music plays. Silence.

Ruth (*referring to the music*) That's me, too.

Beat.

Claudie Don't upset your parents, Carl. You shouldn't do that.

Phone rings again.

(*into phone*) Hello? (*Holds out phone.*) It's your father.

With music playing, Carl takes the phone.

Carl (*hesitates, then into phone*) Dad?

Carl says nothing. Shouting from the phone. He listens, then after a while, with the shouting continuing, he just hangs up. He sits back on the sofa. Claudie and Ruth don't know what to say.

Ruth (*'browsing' through the Kama Sutra*) Can I borrow this sometime?

Carl (*to Claudie*) I want to stay here.

Claudie Think what you're doing.

Carl (*yells*) I know what I'm doing!

Claudie is taken aback by this outburst.

Claudie (*after a glance at Ruth, who still has her head in the book*) You're a wonderful boy. (*She reaches for his hand.*) We've had a lot of fun.

Beat.

You're more than a boy . . . but is it worth it, Carl?

Carl It is.

He refuses her hand. She looks at Ruth, who looks up and nods, as if to say, 'Tell him.'

Claudie You've been so – good to be with. I've enjoyed myself so much. Thank you.

Beat.

Ruth Claudie . . .

Claudie (*looks at Ruth, then*) Ruth is right. I should tell you.

Carl Tell me what?

Claudie Monsieur Darc and I –

The phone starts to ring. They hesitate, but it is clear no one will answer it.

(*continuing as the phone rings*) Monsieur Darc, your mathematics teacher and I – we had an argument this week, Carl . . . (*speaking over the ringing phone*) An awful argument. And we agreed not to see each other – again. See each other – as we have been seeing each other, I mean. I was hurt by this.

Ringing.

Very hurt, Carl. I needed someone. Last night I needed some . . . (*then as the ringing stops*) I don't love you.

Short pause.

Ruth (*referring to the music*) Maybe I should turn this – (*off*)

Claudie No.

She looks at Carl and starts to cry. Carl just looks at her, confused.

(*sniffling*) That's not totally true. What I've just said . . . I . . . (*Rubs her sniffling nose.*) I have hated myself today. Whenever I've allowed myself to think – what do you think you're doing, Claudie, he's . . . I have hated myself. Please go home.

No one moves. Carl stares at Claudie, then:

Carl I'm staying here.

Beat.

Ruth (*suddenly standing*) What about wine? We should have wine if we're having dinner.

Claudie (*wiping her eyes*) There are bottles in the –

Ruth I know where you keep it.

She goes off into the kitchen. Carl has watched her go.

Carl (*to say something*) Ruth looks so different. Than this morning. (*He hands her his handkerchief.*) In that dress. It's like she's another person. Like she's – beautiful. I suppose she is. Before I didn't think she was beautiful at all.

Claudie (*blowing her nose now into the handkerchief*) Women change. And there is a lesson in life, young man,

57

that you will learn something like one or two billion more times.

She smiles and winks at him and hands him back his handkerchief. Phone rings again. They let it ring. Claudie sighs, breathes deeply, and goes and turns up the music, then sits next to Carl on the sofa. The phone ringing stops.

What will he do to you?

He puts her hand on his leg. Ruth enters with a bottle of wine and a corkscrew.

Ruth Here's the wine. Now shouldn't we have our man here open it? It is a man's thing to do.

Claudie 'Please, sir – could you help us girls?'

He takes the bottle and starts to open it.

Ruth Look at those muscles, Claudie.

Claudie I'm looking.

Ruth Us girls couldn't do that.

Claudie (*pushing the joke*) No-o-o-o.

Cork pops.

Carl What shall it be, ladies? (*Holds up the bottle.*) Red or – (*Picks up the crabs medicine.*) – white?

The women are disgusted.

Ruth For a minute there I forget he was thirteen.

Claudie (*'correcting' her*) Twelve.

He pours. Music plays. Ruth pauses as she hears herself play.

Claudie Did you call Robert and tell him about the crabs?

Ruth Why would I –?

Beat.

I did. And he knew. He's known.

The music ends and there is applause on the record. Claudie and then Carl join in the applause.

It's the only record we've made so far. The only piece. The rest of the album's other groups –

Claudie (*to Carl*) I was there. I was in that audience. (*listening to the applause*) There – that's me.

Ruth (*getting the joke*) Shut up. (*She smiles.*)

Applause on the record continues.

Ruth It was quite a night, wasn't it? Everything I'd dreamed of in my clean kitchen in Montclair, New Jersey.

The music continues: another group or soloist.

Claudie I'd never seen an all-girl string quartet before. It seemed really strange, you know. Good but strange. Like – I don't know.

Ruth (*picking up the album cover*) Hélène is the real beauty. Beautiful red hair. That's red hair. (*photo in black and white*) The cellist.

Carl looks at the photo.

Claudie Carl was saying he thinks you're beautiful, Ruth.

Carl is embarrassed.

Carl Why did you – ?

Ruth (*at the same time*) When did – ?

Claudie (*continuing*) When you were – (*Gestures.*) How you look now. Isn't that right?

He says nothing.

Ruth You've put him on the spot.

Claudie (*back to the concert*) I went with Paul. (*to Carl*) Monsieur Darc. And his wife. As sort of a teachers' group. And he said he had never even seen a female cellist before. (*to Carl*) They're hardly in orchestras.

Ruth Women.

Claudie You never see them. (*back to Ruth*) And just watching Helene play, with her thighs, Paul said, wrapped around it – it was, he said, one of the most sensual things he'd ever seen. Or heard.

Beat.

He said this to both me and his wife.

Ruth When I left Monclair and my husband and my baby –

Carl turns on hearing this.

Claudie (*explaining*) She left her baby.

Ruth (*explaining more*) My mother-in-law convinced me she'd be a better mother. (*continuing her story*) My husband laughed in my face. Going to Paris? For Christ's sake, girl, what do you want? I said what I wanted is . . .

Beat.

I'm sure I said something stupid. Something I'd heard. Something I don't believe in any more. Because I suppose I didn't know.

Beat.

But then came that night. (*Gestures toward the album. Pause.*)

Carl (*getting it, to Claudie*) That's when she knew why she –

Claudie I understood.

   Beat.

He beat her, Carl.

Ruth I hit him too. Sometimes I hit him first. I don't blame him for that. I didn't leave for that.

   Claudie picks up the needle to replay Ruth's piece.

Let's not hear it again.

   Claudie picks up the needle again and sets it on the end of Ruth's 'cut'. So we hear only the applause again. They listen to the applause until it ends, drink their wine. Ruth has picked up the Kama Sutra *again.*
   When the applause ends, Claudie begins to put on more music. As she does:

Claudie I'd never let a man hit me.

Ruth (*taking a cigarette from the pack*) Cigarette?

Claudie Please. (*Hands her one.*)

Carl I'd love to come and hear you play.

Claudie Carl has been learning about music. His family doesn't listen to music. So he's practically a virgin.

   Beat.

Practically.

   Beat.

I've promised to take him to *The Magic Flute*.

Ruth When I was about your age. How old is he?

Claudie Fifteen.

Ruth I was fourteen. I got – I asked for and I got a recording of *The Magic Flute* for Christmas.

Carl How did you know even to ask for –?

Ruth I just did. (*continuing*) I played it over and over in my room. On my little portable plastic record player.

Claudie nods. She knows the type.

My friends, they were only interested in – (*Shrugs.*) Elvis Presley? I don't know. In all sorts of things I wasn't interested in at all. That I thought were stupid. That I still think are stupid. My ex – He loved that stuff. He made me dance to it with him. The son of a bitch even laughed at me when I practised. What's that going to get you? What is that – *about*? I felt like a freak in that house. And maybe I was. I'll play for you sometime. (*Smiles at Carl.*)

Carl Thank you.

Claudie Robert, I thought, plays the guitar and . . .

Ruth I wasn't interested in his guitar playing.

They laugh, calm down, then quietly:

Robert and his little tiny friends (*his crabs*). Look at this. I've been looking through this (*the* Kama Sutra). There's – (*Finds the reference.*) 'the widely opened position'. That's me. Completely open.

Claudie I don't think I've read any of the text. I bought it for the pictures. (*Looks at the book.*)

Ruth (*reads*) 'The yawning position.' That's me with my ex. 'The position of the wife of Indra.'

Claudie What is that one? The wife one.

Ruth (*reads*) 'When she places her thighs with her legs doubled on them upon her sides and thus engages in congress.'

Beat.

'This is learnt only by practice.'

Beat.

Claudie Jesus.

Ruth (*continues reading*) 'When a woman forcibly holds in her yoni the lingam after it is in, it is called the "mare's position". This too is learnt by practice only and is chiefly found among the women of the Andra country.'

Claudie (*turning to Carl*) Are you staying the night or . . . ?

Carl I don't know.

Ruth (*reads*) 'When a man supports himself against a wall, and the woman, sitting on his hands joined together and held underneath her, throws her arms around his neck, and putting her thighs alongside his waist, moves herself by her feet, which are touching the wall against which the man is leaning, it is called the "suspended congress".'

Beat.

Claudie (*unable to visualise this*) What???

Ruth hands her the book, pointing at the page.

Claudie There's no picture?

Ruth Not for that one.

Carl sits uncomfortably between them.

Claudie (*reads to herself*) 'When a man against a wall –' Carl, come over to the wall.

Stands, pulling up Carl. He hesitates. He follows her, she reads:

'Against a wall.' (*She positions Carl against the wall.*)
'Woman, sitting on his hands' . . . (*as she joins his hands together*) Like this. (*Reads.*) 'Underneath her.' (*She starts to climb up onto his hands.*) Pick me up. Carl. That's right. 'Arms around the neck – ' Ruth, could you hold the book?

Ruth takes the book

'Thighs alongside his waist.' (*to Ruth*) Like this you think?

Ruth holds out the book for Claudie to read as she starts to climb onto Carl, whose back is pressed against the wall.

'Moves herself by her feet.' (*She is on him, starts to move her feet.*)

Is that right? Did I skip something?

She looks to Ruth, moves her feet. Carl is trying to keep his balance.

(*to Carl*) Keep holding. (*to Ruth*) What does that – ? (*to Carl*) Carl, you're letting me – Carl!

They stumble away from the wall. Claudie calls to Ruth for help, she tries to push him back to the wall, until finally, as Claudie screams, Carl and she fall, laughing.
Carl takes this chance quickly to kiss her – the first time he has.
She realises this and kisses him back.

Claudie (*not a question*) You are staying tonight.

Ruth I think I should go. I –

Claudie No, no, not yet. Please, we were going to eat. What happened to eating?

Ruth I don't think anyone's hungry. I'm not hungry.

Claudie You should eat. Remember you're eating for more than one now.

Ruth Christ.

Carl (*not understanding*) What, is Ruth – ?

Claudie For five or six hundred or more now.

> *Carl realises that it's another joke about the crabs.*

Then let's at least open another bottle of wine. Drink up.

Carl (*the wine bottle is still half full*) We haven't finished –

Claudie We will! I'll get the wine!

> *Claudie goes to the kitchen. Music plays.*
> *Ruth and Carl say nothing for a moment, but they smile at each other.*

Ruth (*finally*) That – (*Carl against the wall*) was funny.

> *Carl nods.*
> *Short pause, then:*

Carl (*as if explaining everything*) She's my teacher.

> *Beat.*
> *They burst out laughing.*
> *Beat.*

Ruth Claudie was telling me about a student of hers who was going to be a poet.

> *This stops him.*

So that's you.

> *Beat.*

You don't have any of your poems – ?

Carl I don't know what I'll be.

Ruth Claudie has tons of poetry books.

Carl I know. I've seen.

Claudie (*entering with wine and cheese*) Where's our man? (*to open the wine*)

Ruth Claudie should show you her writing.

Claudie (*protesting*) Ruth, I'm not going to show –

Ruth (*to Carl*) She's writing a novel.

Carl You never said –

Claudie (*over this*) What literature teacher hasn't tried to write a novel? Choose some music.

Ruth Show him. He'd be interested –

Claudie Carl, you choose –

Carl I don't know what to –

Ruth (*over this*) You want to know what it's about? It's about –

Claudie Don't tell him! (*Covers his ears.*) It sounds stupid talking about it.

    Beat.

Ruth It's interesting.

Carl I'm sure it –

Claudie Open the wine, young man. (*trying to change and subject and make a joke*) Earn your keep. Make up for your inability to perform – what was it called in the book?

    No response. Carl and Ruth just look at her.

(*to Ruth*) Why did you bring that up?

Ruth (*to Carl*) I'll choose some music.

She takes the job away from a reluctant Carl. She will put something quiet on – piano music.
   Pause.

Claudie (*finally*) Okay. Every student should get at least once the chance to laugh at his teacher. (*She heads off to her bedroom.*)

Carl I won't laugh.

The music is on. Claudie returns with a box of papers and sets them down. Carl has just opened the bottle of wine.

Claudie (*holding out her glass to Carl*) I need a drink for this.

He pours.

It takes place, of course, in the Middle Ages.

Carl Why 'of course'?

Ruth Because it's about –

Claudie Sh–sh.

Beat.

Ruth She's done a lot of research and –

Claudie Ruth.

Beat.

A specific period: November 1429 to about the next March, 1430. Four and a half months. Mostly in a large barn, it's actually a workshop attached to a convent – outside Paris. A group of women, mostly nuns – but nuns at this time, it's complicated. Here is where they paint. You've seen – I showed you a couple today, Carl – the manuscripts painted, called illuminated manuscripts.

Did you know that many of these – all of which are
attributed to monks, to this monastery or that order
of monks – were in truth painted by women?

Beat.

Sort of 'farmed out' art. To different convents – who
got no credit but a little money from the monks – who
got a lot more from – whomever was paying.

Beat.

So some of the nuns here – well, their major skill was
painting and so pretty much anyone could be a nun if
they painted well – that was *the* qualification – so you
could in fact *be* other things. You couldn't be married,
but you could have men. You could have children. But
you were a nun.

Beat.

Into this barn, one day, comes a man in a suit of armour.
A short man. Visor down, staggering under the weight of
the metal. The women, seeing the soldier and fearing the
worst, try and flee, but a voice calls out from inside the
armour:
'Stop. Please. I'm not here to hurt you.'
And the soldier falls to the dirt ground. One of the
women goes to him, hesitantly, and in removing the
helmet realises – the man is a woman.

Ruth The most famous woman –

Claudie Jeanne d'Arc.

Beat.

Let me backtrack for a second. By the autumn of 1429,
Jeanne d'Arc was without doubt the most famous
woman in France – in the world maybe, but certainly
in France. She'd helped us capture Orleans, and helped

crown the Dauphin. Because of this her movements are well documented – part of history. A day-by-day account of what she did, where she was – can be put together. (*She sips, then:*) Until November 1429. And for the next four months. With the sole exception of a single visit to Orleans where she was seen by others only at a distance, and from a balcony. Except for this – Jeanne's whereabouts are unknown. As are the reasons for her disappearance. All this is true.

Beat.

So it is Jeanne d'Arc on this dirt ground, in the convent's barn. And why is she here, Carl? Because – she's pregnant.

Phone rings. They hesitate, then Claudie nods to Ruth, who gets up and gets it.

Ruth (*into phone*) Hello? It's Ruth. (*She turns to Claudie.*) It's Paul.

Carl is relieved, thinking of course it was his father.

Claudie I'm busy.

Ruth looks at her.

I am busy.

Ruth (*into phone*) She's busy. (*Hangs up.*)

Claudie (*after another drink, then*) The Maid of Orleans, the virgin princess, this woman whose very purity is the definition of France – has fallen.

Beat.

She is taken in. Allowed to sleep in the hay. She grows larger. For a long time she won't speak. The women, one day, get her to pose, naked, pregnant, for a painting of the Virgin Mary. They needed a model.

Beat.

She will say nothing of the father. She is still obsessed with her own purity. 'What does that' – her bulging stomach – asks one of the women, 'have to do with purity?' This particular woman was a very fine painter and a nun in name only.

Beat.

Finally – and I'm skipping way ahead now – the Dauphin's people find her. That's when she has to go to Orleans and hide behind the railing on the balcony.

Beat.

The Dauphin's people are shocked. They predict the fall of France. Scholars are brought in and there is a movement to declare it an immaculate conception and the Child of God. The brother – or sister – of Jesus. This is debated and the debate takes two months. Meanwhile Jeanne is allowed to return to the barn and the nuns. And there, in March 1430, she gives birth, with profound pain, to a baby girl.

Short pause.

The next day she puts her armour back on and returns to the Dauphin's side, where she stayed, until being captured and burnt at the stake.

Beat.

It's a story about a lot of things, but mostly I think it's about a woman who risks everything to have a child she knows she doesn't want.

Beat.

I've been pregnant three times. But I have no child.

Pause.

(*quietly*) The last was your mathematics teacher's. (*She fiddles with the pages of the manuscript.*) It's not finished. (*She closes the box top and suddenly to change the subject and mood she grabs the* Kama Sutra, *quickly finds a page and reads*.) 'When after congress has begun the woman places one of her legs on her lover's shoulder and stretches the other out –'

Carl starts to open the box of papers.

Claudie Don't read it.

Carl closes the top. Ruth who is still by the albums suddenly holds one up:

Ruth (*showing Claudie*) Claudie?

Claudie (*smiling*) Why not? He knows everything else about us.

Carl is curious now.

Ruth (*to Carl*) You heard this? 'Les Djinns Singers.'

Carl No, who –?

Ruth My brother gave this to me as a going-away present. He meant it as a joke, but we love it, don't we?

Claudie (*taking the album and reading the title*) 'Sixty French Girls Can't Be Wrong!'

As Claudie puts it on –

Carl Why is it – (*here*)?

Ruth My record player's been broken for –

Claudie (*reading the back of the album*) 'From Paris, come these sixty Princesses, to raise their voices in exuberant and sentimental song in a dozen varied selections.'

Ruth (*jumps up and reads*) 'What makes these renditions all the more outstanding is the fact that the entire assemblage consists of' –

Both – 'jeune filles' –

Claudie – 'between the ages of thirteen and sixteen!'

Ruth Your age, Carl!

Claudie 'Each youngster was especially auditioned and selected on the basis of personal qualification and aptitude, and after an – unusually exacting audition.' Bite your tongue, Ruth.

> *Claudie puts the needle down on the song 'Oui Oui Oui' – sung by these sixty jeune filles. It is silly and kitsch. As soon as the music starts or just a fraction before, Claudie and Ruth form a 'line' and mouth along. Doing a dance number they have worked out – obviously they have done this many times before.*
> *Carl watches, smiling. The women can barely keep a straight face.*

Claudie (*as they dance*) I think we've been alone together too many Saturday nights!

> *As the song plays, Carl has picked up the album to read it. Suddenly Claudie hurries to her bedroom.*

Claudie (*rushing off*) I'll be right back. Right back.

Ruth I know what she's going to get.

> *As the song plays, Ruth opens a small drawer in a table and takes out a small bag of marijuana and some wrappers.*

Ruth (*to Carl*) Do you smoke grass?

> *Claudie runs out of her bedroom putting on white socks. She has another pair for Ruth.*

Claudie (*explaining*) To make us – jeune – (*Sees what Ruth is doing, almost says something, then doesn't.*) Sixty-two French girls can't be wrong.

72

Ruth (*taking the socks*) I'm not French.

Claudie In spirit you are! (*Then she has to say something.*) He doesn't smoke dope.

Ruth How do you know? (*to Carl*) You smoke dope?

Carl Sure.

> *Song continues. Ruth has put her white socks on and grabs Carl and dances with him. Claudie is left to roll the joint. As she does, she watches the two dance. Ruth starts to get quite close to Carl.*

Claudie (*finally, after having rolled the joint*) Ruth, stop it. That's enough.

> *Claudie stops the music. She hands the joint to Ruth, who lights it.*

(*to Carl*) As I said, too many Saturdays alone together. Come here.

> *She sits. He joins her. Ruth hands Claudie the joint. Claudie takes a puff, then leans over and kisses Carl, opening his mouth with hers and blowing the smoke into him. She then hands him the joint, and he tries to do the same to her, but starts to cough. As he gets better:*

Carl (*seemingly out of the blue, but it has been on his mind*) There is one poem I think I remember. I could recite it if . . .

> *Short pause. The women listen.*

(*recites*) 'Rhythms –'

Claudie Stand up, Carl.

> *He hesitates, then stands. The ladies, still smoking, curl up on their seats and get ready to listen, catching looks at each other.*

Carl (*recites*)
   'Rhythms silent and frail
   of delicate air
   to catch the curling of hair.

   'Voice crisp and curt,
   O delicate voice,
   curling the catching air.

   'Silent hands
   catch the delicate rhythms
   from the frail hair,
   the silent and the frail hair.'

   Beat.

Ruth (*turns to Claudie*) Is it about you?

Claudie It's good. It is.

Ruth Is that all that you –

Carl It's the first part of something a lot longer. I couldn't recite the rest. (*then, to change the mood and subject*) Let's put back on 'Oui Oui Oui –'.

Ruth (*suddenly standing and interrupting*) I'll get my fiddle. I feel like playing. I'll be right back.

   She goes off. They watch her go, then:

Claudie She doesn't play for everyone. I've tried so many times to –

Carl I'm flattered.

Claudie I loved your poem.

   Carl looks at her, then goes to the record player.

Carl While we're waiting. (*He puts on 'Oui Oui Oui' or another kitschy song from the 'Sixty French Girls Can't Be Wrong' album.*)

Claudie It was brave of you to recite it. (*She gets up and goes up behind him. She strokes his hair as the music begins to play. Grabbing the hair that falls in his face*) God, I wish I could cut this off.

Carl's father, a large man in his forties, enters from the hallway, at first unseen. Carl turns away to Claudie and sees his father.

Father The door was open.

Carl (*in shock*) Father –

Claudie Monsieur –

Father Madame Melville. 'Madame' with no husband. I spoke with the headmaster.

The music plays.

Carl, let's go.

He doesn't move.

Let's go, Carl.

Ruth enters behind him with her violin. Then Father goes to Carl and with neither saying a word, he reaches around and picks Carl up around the waist and begins carrying him out like a child.

Carl, without words or sound, fights, kicks like a little boy having a tantrum. As they struggle, Carl kicks the sofa, kicks objects off a table.

The two women can barely look. Claudie suddenly tries to stop the music – and drags the needle over the record, scratching it.

Now there is only silence and father and son struggle. Only their breathing is heard, until finally, after a great effort, Father carries his child off.

Pause.

Neither woman says anything. Ruth begins absent-mindedly to pluck her violin strings.

Lights shift and Carl returns and speaks to the audience, as the women slowly fade away. He carries a small pile of clothes.

Carl I was taken out of the ironically named American School immediately, and arrangements were made to send me back to Ohio to live with my aunts.

Beat.

I saw Mme Melville again only once. The night before my departure, Father and Mother took me to a restaurant for dinner. I requested something on the Left Bank, near the Sorbonne. Father was suspicious. But Mother, already upset that I was leaving, and missing me terribly, agreed to whatever I wished.

Beat.

We ordered. I went to wash my hands in the WC, and kept running. I figured Father would know where I went, but I also figured he wouldn't bring Mother with him, nor could he leave her in the restaurant alone. This was France after all. So he'd drive her home first and this gave me time.

Beat.

She wore a short, tight, black dress.

Claudie enters and he hands her the black dress and she begins to undress and put it on.

I wore a suit that I thought made me look old.

Carl begins to undress and put the suit on. For a moment then, they are both in their underwear. They look and smile at each other, then put on their new clothes, with a little help – a zipper, a collar – from the other.

When I arrived, she told me she had a date for that night, so I couldn't stay long. We sat together on the sofa. She put on music.

Claudie puts on an album.

Carl What are you –?

Claudie *The Magic Flute.*

It is the 'Papagena! Papagenia!' duet. They listen. Claudie takes off her shoes and curls up next to him. He looks at her.

Carl (*about the music*) What are they – (*saying*)?

Claudie They love each other. They want to be together.

Beat.

Listen.

She touches him to get him focusing on a moment in the music.
They listen.
She touches his leg apparently by accident. He notices.

Excuse me.

She moves her hand. She looks up at him, then away.
Doorbell. He looks at her. She ignores it. They listen until the song is over and the record clicks off.

Carl (*to audience*) She asked me to stay until after she'd gone. She said she didn't want Paul, Monsieur Darc, my math teacher, to see me here.

Silence.
Claudie leans over and slips on her shoes. She stands and holds out her hand so Carl can steady her balance as she adjusts her shoes.

She looks at him, then turns and looks at the back of her skirt.

Claudie Is it smooth?

He nods.

No wrinkles?

He shakes his head.
She straightens the skirt anyway.
Slowly she walks toward the door. He watches her walk. She again runs her hand along her behind, to straighten out any wrinkles.
Carl continues to watch.
As she approaches the door, she turns back to him and, with only the tips of her fingers, she waves good-bye and is gone.
From the hallway we hear the door opening, a brief conversation, and the door closing.
Pause.

Carl Years later. And years and years ago. When I was twenty-four, I ran into a friend from my Paris days. And he told me Mme Melville had died.

Beat.

Of cancer, he thought.

Pause.

Carl (*to the air*) May I see that good-bye one more time?

Beat.
Claudie returns (there is no sound of the door opening). She goes to the sofa and sits, taking off her shoes and placing them just where they were before.
She leans against Carl.
She leans over and slips on her shoes. She stands and holds out her hand so Carl can steady her balance as she adjusts her shoes.

78

She looks at him, then turns and looks at the back of her skirt.

Claudie Is it smooth?

He nods.

No wrinkles?

He shakes his head.
  She straightens the skirt anyway.
  Slowly she walks toward the door. He watches her walk. She again runs her hand along her behind, to straighten out any wrinkles.
  Carl continues to watch.
  As she approaches the door, she turns back to him and, with only the tips of her fingers, she waves good-bye and is gone.
  From the hallway we hear the door opening, a brief conversation, and the door closing.
  Pause.
  Carl turns away from the door, stands, and walks off the stage in the opposite direction.
  End of play.